300-Calorie or Less

Naturally Delicious Light Meal Ideas

Table of Contents

Zucchini Salad with Sundried Tomato Sauce

Spicy Tuna Tartare

Tilapia Ceviche

Spicy Kale with Poached Eggs

Smoked Salmon Bites

Basil Shrimp

Turkey Apple Wraps

Creamy Cauliflower Soup

Pineapple Jicama Salad

Sliced Veggie Spicy Chicken

No-Crust Pepper Quiche

Uptown Clam Chowder

Chicken & Kale Soup

Sweet Guava Salad

Carrot Cranberry Crunch Salad

Introduction

Low-calorie cooking is an art. When trying to create meals around a specific calorie budget, you can no longer throw a bunch of ingredients together based solely on how the final dish is going to taste. With this realization comes the fact that fettuccini Alfredo and meat lovers' pizza are off-limits for a low-calorie dieter. For inexperienced low-calorie dieters, the solution is often very simple: have a salad. Yet, a large salad with chicken, cheese, croutons and creamy dressing can contain 600-800 calories. Instead, try one of our alternative soup, salad or light meal options. They all contain 300 calories or less, but don't let that fool you into thinking you'll be eating "rabbit food". Our recipes let you enjoy nuts, olive oil, and –yes– bacon! The key is to balance them out with low-cal greens.

Forget the store-bought salad dressing and dive into the world of flavorful, healthy low-calorie cooking. This book features recipes loaded with veggies, fruits, lean meats and eggs for endless possibilities. Begin your journey to mastering the art of low-cal cooking or simply add another set of recipes to your low-cal cooking arsenal!

Why 300-Calorie Recipes?

For some people, eating 3 square meals a day is not optimal for various reasons. To keep blood sugar stable, eating 6 smaller, 300-calorie meals per day is a popular option. By eating small meals, insulin spikes are kept under control, and blood sugar levels never drop because the body constantly receives food. This small-meal approach is used by many people who are physically active in order to sustain energy throughout the day. Some will prefer to have 3 small meals and a larger one, allowing for a greater variety of flavors and nutrients.

If you're looking at a 300-cal meal plan, there are a few things you need to know. Ideally, you will vary the foods from one meal to the other in order to get a wide array of nutrients. Eating 300 calories' worth of one food in one sitting, then eating 300 calories' worth of another food 2 hours later will likely cause you to miss out on vital nutrients found in a variety of foods. Creating simple yet nourishing 300-calorie meals is an art; balancing macronutrients (fat, protein and carbohydrates) along with micronutrients (vitamins, antioxidants and minerals) is the key to a successful 300-calorie meal.

Because some foods are very high in calories, they need to be avoided or consumed with moderation when aiming for 300-calorie meals. Nuts, avocado, oils, sugar, starches, grains, cheese and fatty meats such as bacon need to be limited because even a small amount of these foods will quickly burn through a 300-cal budget. The priority goes to chicken breast, eggs, lean fish, fruits, veggies and a little amount of fat. Soups, egg dishes and salads make excellent 300-calorie meals, but even stir-fries can be redesigned to fit the low-calorie guideline. Replacing the rice with grated cauliflower or swapping noodles for low-cal kelp noodles are creative ways to enjoy some waistline-friendly favorites.

The recipes in this book pack a ton of nutrition into a low-calorie package. You can enjoy each of them as part of a low-calorie wellness plan. If you wish, you can pair some of the soup options with a small spinach side salad drizzled with lemon juice or apple cider vinegar and a drop of olive oil for a complete low-calorie meal. Have fun experimenting with various combinations to create your own delicious and healthy meals!

Foods to Avoid

No food is off-limits, but you will generally want to avoid or limit:

- Pre-packaged foods: meal replacement bars, low-calorie frozen dinners and stuff that comes out of a can are not the best way to meet your daily nutrient needs. Loaded with sugar and preservatives, those foods leave you unsatisfied. Low-calorie prepared dinners are only low-cal because they come in tiny portions.

- Sugar: all sugar is high in calories and should be avoided. One tablespoon of honey adds 64 calories to your meal.

- Oils and fats: extra virgin oils such as olive and coconut oils can actually be consumed in moderation, even on a low-cal diet. While they are very high in calories, these fats contribute to good health in various ways. One tablespoon of oil contains upwards of 100 calories, so make sure you go easy. Avoid industrial and vegetable oils, avoid deep-fried anything, and save the oil for sautéing or as a salad garnish.

- Grains: grains have an obvious disadvantage when it comes to calories. They are made up of starches and sugars and their water content is relatively low, making them extremely high in calories. One cup of cooked pasta contains almost 200 calories, and not many people limit themselves to such a small amount. Likewise, 2 slices of wheat bread provide the same amount of calories, leaving very little room for extra nutrients.

- Cheese, avocado: while these foods are healthy, their calorie count adds up quickly. It's best to limit them. Sprinkle a spoonful of shredded cheese or add a bit of avocado to a salad for an extra treat, but try to go easy.

- Most meats and fish: eating small amounts of meat and fish is healthy. Problems arise when you eat half a pound of regular ground beef or fatty fish since the calorie count can be upwards of 1500 per pound. Focus on skinless white chicken meat, rabbit, lean fish and turkey, and swap regular sausage for turkey sausage. Limit meat to small servings, since a meat-based meal will generally be high in calories. One boneless, skinless chicken breast provides 260 cals. Make a meal for two out of the same piece of meat by stir-frying it with bok choy, celery, onions and peppers. Bacon can be enjoyed as a condiment at 40 calories per slice.

- Alcohol: it provides no nutrients and contains huge amounts of calories.

- Condiments: mayonnaise, ketchup, aioli, sweet relish, pesto, guacamole and honey mustard taste delicious, but they will quickly fill up a calorie budget. Instead, try some lemon juice, fresh salsa, fresh herbs or sauerkraut to top your dishes.

- Nuts: high in all kinds of nutrients, nuts are also extremely high in calories and fat. They can be enjoyed in moderation in salads or sprinkled on creamy vegetable soups.

Creamy Parsnip Soup

Prep Time: 10 minutes

Cook Time: 25 minutes

Servings: 4

INGREDIENTS

1 large yellow onion, chopped

2 ripe pears, peeled and chopped

6 parsnips, peeled and chopped

4 cups chicken or vegetable broth

2 Tablespoons olive oil

1 teaspoon sea salt

INSTRUCTIONS

1. Sauté onion in olive oil in a large stockpot over medium-high heat until translucent.
2. Add parsnips, pears, broth, and salt.
3. Cover and bring to a boil.
4. Reduce heat to medium and simmer for approximately 20 minutes, until parsnips are tender.
5. Puree the soup with a hand blender, or in batches in a blender or food processor.

Chicken Soup

Prep Time: 10 minutes

Cook Time: 40 minutes

Servings: 4

INGREDIENTS

1 large yellow onion, chopped

4 garlic cloves, minced

2 carrots, chopped

2 stalks of celery, chopped

1 cup sliced mushrooms

½ cup parsley, chopped

4 cups chicken broth

2 skinless chicken legs

2 skinless chicken thighs

2 Tablespoons olive oil

1 teaspoon sea salt

INSTRUCTIONS

1. Sauté onion and garlic in olive oil in a large stockpot over medium heat until translucent.

2. Add the celery, carrots, and mushrooms and cook, stirring, for about 5 minutes.

3. Add the chicken legs and thighs, broth, parsley, and salt. Cover and simmer for 30 minutes.

Emerald Soup

Prep Time: 10 minutes

Cook Time: 25 minutes

Servings: 4

INGREDIENTS

2 large leeks, sliced

2 Tablespoons fresh ginger, grated

4 garlic cloves, minced

2 cups Chinese cabbage, chopped

4 cups fresh spinach

4 cups chicken or vegetable broth

2 Tablespoons coconut oil

1 teaspoon sea salt

INSTRUCTIONS

1. Sauté leeks in coconut oil in a large stockpot over medium-high heat about 5 minutes.
2. Add ginger and garlic, and stir, cooking, for another minute.
3. Add the cabbage, broth, and salt. Cover, and simmer for 20 minutes.
4. Add the spinach and stir in until wilted.

Quick Chicken Stir-Fry

Prep Time: 15 minutes

Cook Time: 20 minutes

Servings: 4

INGREDIENTS

1 pound chicken meat, cut into 1-inch chunks

1 yellow onion, sliced

2 carrots, peeled and sliced thinly

4 cups baby bok choy (about 2 heads), chopped

12 ounces mushrooms, halved

4 Tablespoons coconut oil

4 cloves garlic, chopped

1 Tablespoon grated ginger

1 Tablespoon apple cider vinegar.

1 teaspoon sea salt

INSTRUCTIONS

1. Sauté onions in coconut oil in a deep sauté pan or wok for about 3 minutes, or until translucent.
2. Add the chicken and cook, stirring frequently, until lightly browned.
3. Add the bok choy, carrots, and mushrooms and continue to sauté for a few minutes.
4. In a separate bowl, mix the vinegar, garlic, ginger, and salt, and whisk until blended.

5. Pour the sauce over the chicken and vegetables and cook, stirring frequently until vegetables are crisp-tender.

Potato-free Leek Soup

Prep Time: 15 minutes

Cook Time: 40 minutes

Servings: 4

INGREDIENTS

1 large yellow onion, chopped

2 large leeks, cleaned and sliced

1 large rutabaga, peeled and chopped

1 large head cauliflower, cored and chopped

6 cups chicken broth

2 Tablespoons olive oil

4 strips bacon (optional)

1 teaspoon sea salt

INSTRUCTIONS

1. Sauté onion in olive oil in a large stockpot over medium-high heat until translucent (about 4 minutes).
2. Add the leeks to the pot and cook, stirring, until lightly browned.
3. Add the rutabaga, cauliflower, salt, and stock to the pot. Bring to a boil.
4. Reduce heat to low, cover, and simmer for 30 minutes, until rutabaga is cooked through.
5. Puree the soup with a hand blender, or blender.

Healthy Caesar Salad

Prep Time: 5 minutes

Cook Time: 12 minutes

Servings: 2

INGREDIENTS

2 Tablespoons olive oil

2 Tablespoons lemon juice

4 anchovies

4 slices of bacon, diced

1 clove garlic, minced

4 cups romaine lettuce, torn

1 cup radicchio, torn

INSTRUCTIONS

1. Heat 1 Tablespoon oil in a skillet and sauté bacon until cooked, about 4-5 minutes.
2. In a blender or food processor, combine the remaining oil, the anchovies, and the lemon juice.
3. In a large bowl, toss the lettuce with the dressing and bacon.

Sweet Potato Shepherd's Pie

Prep Time: 10 minutes

Cook Time: 50 minutes

Servings: 4

INGREDIENTS

1 pound extra-lean ground turkey

1 large onion, chopped

2 medium zucchini, chopped

2 large sweet potatoes, peeled and diced

1 teaspoon dried thyme

1 teaspoon dried basil

2 Tablespoons olive oil

1 teaspoon sea salt

INSTRUCTIONS

1. Brown the meat with the onion in a large skillet. Cook until meat is fully cooked, about 15-20 minutes.
2. In another stockpot, steam sweet potatoes for about 20 minutes.
3. Add the zucchini and spices to the meat and cook for another 5 minutes.
4. Preheat oven to 400 °F.
5. Drain the sweet potatoes and return them to the pot. Mash with a potato masher and mix in the olive oil and sea salt.
6. Transfer the meat to a large casserole pan and pat it down with a spatula.

7. Spoon the mashed sweet potatoes on top of the meat, and spread it evenly across the pan.

8. Bake for 30 minutes.

Cream of Broccoli Soup

Prep Time: 10 minutes

Cook Time: 25 minutes

Servings: 4

INGREDIENTS

1 large yellow onion, chopped

2 large turnips, peeled and chopped

1 head broccoli, chopped

4 cups chicken or vegetable broth

2 Tablespoons olive oil

1 teaspoon sea salt

INSTRUCTIONS

1. Sauté onion in olive oil in a large stockpot over medium-high heat until translucent.
2. Add turnips, broccoli, stock, and salt. Cover and bring to a boil.
3. Reduce heat to medium-low and simmer for approximately 20 minutes, until turnips are tender.
4. Puree the soup with a hand blender, or in batches in a blender or food processor.

Sweet and Sour Chicken

Prep Time: 10 minutes

Cook Time: 20 minutes

Servings: 4

INGREDIENTS

1 pound skinless chicken breasts, cut into cubes

1 bunch scallions, chopped

1 cup pineapple, chopped (fresh or frozen)

2 large carrots, thinly sliced

2 stalks celery, sliced

½ pound mushrooms, halved

¼ cup apple cider vinegar

2 tablespoons coconut oil

1-inch piece of ginger, peeled and minced

2 cloves garlic, minced

INSTRUCTIONS

1. In a large skillet or walk, sauté the onions, celery, and garlic in the oil until soft, about 2 minutes.

2. Add the carrots, the mushrooms, the pineapple, and the chicken and continue stir-frying another 5 minutes.

3. Add the vinegar, cover, and reduce heat to low for 10 minutes.

Asparagus with Prosciutto

Prep Time: 10 minutes

Cook Time: 20 minutes

Servings: 4

INGREDIENTS

1 bunch asparagus, trimmed

2 Tablespoons plus 1 teaspoon olive oil

8 ounces prosciutto, thinly sliced

½ teaspoon sea salt

INSTRUCTIONS

1. Preheat oven to 400 °F.
2. Divide the asparagus spears into 8 bundles.
3. Wrap each bundle with 1/8 of the prosciutto and place on a baking sheet, lightly greased with 1 teaspoon olive oil.
4. Drizzle the remaining olive oil over the bundles and sprinkle with salt.
5. Bake for about 20 minutes, until asparagus is tender.

Spicy Kale Quiche

Prep time: 10 minutes

Cook time: 15 minutes

Serves: 4

INGREDIENTS

8 cage-free eggs

2 tbsp extra virgin olive oil

1 7oz bag of Kale greens

1 shallot

¼ tsp chipotle chili pepper powder

2 cloves garlic

½ lemon

2 tbsp coconut oil

¼ tbsp ground black pepper

INSTRUCTIONS

1. Place a steamer basket in the bottom of a large pot and fill with water; if you see water rise above the bottom of the basket, pour some out. Bring the water to a boil.
2. Wash the kale and remove the stems. Mince the garlic and shallot and squeeze the juice from the lemon into a bowl.

3. In a large pan, add the eggs and extra virgin olive oil. Mixing in the chipotle chili pepper powder, scramble the eggs, breaking them up until they form many small pieces, tender yet firm.
4. Place the kale in the pot and steam until tender and bright-green.
5. Remove the kale from the pot and combine with the eggs. Add the garlic, shallot and lemon juice, drizzle the coconut oil over top and add the ground black pepper. Mix and stir thoroughly.
6. Serve immediately or chill 20 minutes and then serve.

Eggplant with Pesto Topping

Prep time: 10 minutes

Cook time: 8 minutes

Serves: 4

INGREDIENTS

1 large, thick eggplant

6-8 tomatoes

4 tbsp olive oil

¼ cup fresh basil

2 cloves garlic

INSTRUCTIONS

1. Preheat the grill. Slice the eggplant lengthwise into ½" thick slices, or ensuring that you have 4 slices. Slice the tomatoes into ¼" thick slices. Combine 4 tbsp olive oil with basil and garlic in a food processor and puree together.
2. Grill the eggplant until browned, turning once, about 3-4 minutes per side.
3. Remove eggplant from the grill and lay the tomato slices out over each piece. Top with the pesto puree and serve.

Chilled Mango Soup

Prep Time: 10 minutes

Servings: 4

INGREDIENTS

3 large ripe mangoes

1 large onion (yellow, white or sweet)

2 inch piece fresh ginger

2 chili peppers

Cold water

INSTRUCTIONS

1. Peel mangoes, then carefully slice around pit. Peel and grate ginger. Peel and roughly chop onion. Remove stems and seeds from chilis, if desired.
2. Add to food processor or high-speed blender and process until smooth, about 2 minutes. Add enough water to reach desired consistency.
3. Transfer to serving dish and serve chilled.

Mexican Tomato Soup

Prep Time: 10 minutes

Cook Time: 40 minutes

Servings: 4

INGREDIENTS

2 cans (14.5 oz) organic crushed tomatoes

2 cans (11.5) organic tomato juice

5 large tomatoes (or 10 plum tomatoes)

1/2 cup chicken stock

1 red bell pepper (or 1/4 cup roasted red peppers, jarred)

1/4 red onion (or yellow or white onion)

2 garlic cloves

1/2 Serrano chili pepper (or other chili pepper) (optional)

1 tablespoon tapioca flour (or arrowroot powder)

2 tablespoons fresh Mexican oregano (or 1 teaspoon dried oregano)

2 large basil leaves

1 teaspoon fresh cracked black pepper (or ground black pepper)

Celtic sea salt, to taste

1 small bunch cilantro (for garnish)

2 tablespoons ghee (or bacon fat, cacao butter, or coconut oil)

INSTRUCTIONS
1. Juice tomatoes and set aside.

2. Roast red bell pepper over stove burner or until broiler, if using. Turn to char on all sides until skins sears. Rub off blackened skin. Cut in half and remove seeds, stem and veins.

3. Heat medium pot over medium-high heat. Add fat to hot pot.

4. Peel onion and garlic. Dice onion, roasted and red pepper. Mince garlic and Serrano pepper (optional). Add to hot oiled pot and sauté until fragrant, about 2 minutes.

5. Add tapioca and chicken stock. Stir to combine. Let cook about 2 minutes.

6. Chiffon (thinly slice) basil. Add to pot with tomato juice, crushed tomatoes, oregano, pepper and salt, to taste. Stir to combine.

7. Bring to simmer, then reduce heat to low. Simmer and reduce about 30 minutes, or until desired consistency is reached.

8. Transfer to serving dish. Chop cilantro and sprinkle over dish for garnish.

9. Serve hot.

Spicy Mango Fried Rice

Prep Time: 10 minutes

Cook Time: 15 minutes

Servings: 4

INGREDIENTS

1 head cauliflower

8 oz boneless, skinless chicken

1 mango

1 hot chili pepper

2 scallions

2 garlic cloves

3 tablespoons pure fish sauce (or coconut aminos)

3 teaspoons sesame oil (or walnut or almond oil)

1/2 teaspoon red pepper flake

1/2 lime

Coconut oil (for cooking)

INSTRUCTIONS

1. Heat large skillet or medium cast-iron wok over high heat. Lightly coat with coconut oil.

2. Cut cauliflower into florets and add to food processor with shredding attachment to rice. Or finely mince cauliflower.

3. Peel garlic and ginger and mince. Mince chili pepper. Thinly slice scallions. Carefully peel and dice mango. Dice chicken.

4. Add diced chicken, garlic, ginger, chili pepper and red pepper flake to hot skillet or wok. Sauté until chicken is golden brown and just cooked, about 3 minutes. Remove chicken and set aside.

5. Add cauliflower to hot pan or wok. Sauté about 5 minutes, until cauliflower is golden and a bit softened.

Kelp Noodle Salad

Prep Time: 5 minutes

Cook Time: 5 minutes

Servings: 2

INGREDIENTS

1 package (12 oz) kelp noodles

1/2 lemon

1 small cucumber

1 small red bell pepper

1 large carrot

Small bunch cilantro

2 large basil leaves

Orange Avocado Dressing

1 avocado

1 large orange

1/2 lemon

5 large basil leaves

1/4 teaspoon ground black pepper

1/4 teaspoon cayenne pepper or red pepper flake (optional)

Large bunch cilantro

INSTRUCTIONS

1. Rinse and drain kelp noodles. Add to medium bowl and soak 5 minutes in warm water and juice of 1/2 lemon. Or bring medium

pot of water with juice of 1/2 lemon to a boil and cook kelp
noodles for 5 minutes, if softer texture preferred.

2. Peel, seed and cut cucumber in half width-wise. Cut bell pepper in
    half, then remove stem, seeds and veins. Use vegetable peeler or
    grater to make long, thin slices of carrot. Thinly slice cucumber
    and bell pepper lengthwise.

3. Add veggies and drained kelp noodles to medium mixing bowl.

4. For *Orange Avocado Dressing*, add basil and cilantro leaves to
    food processor or bullet blender with juice of orange and process
    to break down leaves. Slice avocado in half and remove pit. Scoop
    flesh into processor with juice of 1/2 lemon, black pepper and hot
    pepper (optional). Process until thick and until creamy.

5. Pour *Orange Avocado Dressing* over sliced veggies and kelp
    noodles. Toss to coat.

6. Serve immediately. Or refrigerate for 20 minutes and serve chilled.

Zucchini Salad with Sundried Tomato Sauce

Prep Time: 20 minutes*

Servings: 2

INGREDIENTS

1 medium zucchini

1 tomato

5 sundried tomatoes

1 garlic clove

2 fresh basil leaves

1 tablespoon raw virgin coconut oil (or 2 tablespoons warm water)

1/4 teaspoon ground white pepper (or black pepper)

1/4 teaspoon sea salt

INSTRUCTIONS

1. Run zucchini through spiralizer, slice into long, thin shreds with knife, or use vegetable peeler to make flat, thin slices. Sprinkle with a pinch of salt and pepper, and gently toss to coat.

2. Add tomato, sundried tomatoes, peeled garlic, basil, coconut oil or warm water, and remaining salt and pepper to food processor or bullet blender. Process until sauce of desired consistency forms.

3. Transfer zucchini pasta to serving bowls. Top with tomato sauce and serve immediately.

4. Or refrigerate for 20 minutes and serve chilled.

Spicy Tuna Tartare

Prep Time: 15* minutes

Servings: 4

INGREDIENTS

1 lb tuna steak (sushi grade)

1 small cucumber

1 ripe avocado

1 lime

1 garlic clove

1 hot chile pepper

2 tablespoons raw virgin coconut oil

Small bunch fresh cilantro

1 teaspoon red pepper flake

1 teaspoon sea salt

INSTRUCTIONS

1. Peel, seed and dice cucumber and avocado. Finely chop cilantro. Add to medium mixing bowl.

2. Remove seeds, stem and veins from hot pepper. Peel garlic and add to food processor or bullet blender with cayenne and hot pepper. Process until smooth paste forms. Add to bowl.

3. Dice tuna, discarding any tough white gristle. Add to bowl.

4. Squeeze on lime juice and add salt.

5. Gently toss with soft spatula or large spoon.

6. Serve immediately. Or refrigerate 20 minutes and serve chilled.

Tilapia Ceviche

Prep Time: 25 minutes

Servings: 4

INGREDIENTS

1 lb fresh, wild caught skinless tilapia fillets

Juice of 4 limes

Juice of 1 lemon

1 plum tomato

1/2 cucumber

1/2 small red onion

Medium bunch cilantro leaves

1/2 teaspoon sea salt

1/2 teaspoon ground black pepper

1 avocado

1 jalapeño pepper (optional)

INSTRUCTIONS

1. Dice fish with sharp knife. Freeze for 20 minutes to make cutting easier and cleaner, if preferred.

2. Add fish to medium mixing bowl. Juice all limes and 1/2 lemon over fish. Gently mix to combine. Cover and chill in refrigerator for 15 to 20 minutes, until fish is opaque.

3. Drain off liquid from fish and discard. Set fish aside.

4. Seed and dice tomato. Peel and dice cucumber and onion. Stem, seed and vein jalapeño pepper, then mince. Finely chop cilantro.

5. Add everything to marinated fish with salt and pepper. Juice remaining 1/2 lemon and mix to combine.

6. Slice avocado in half and pit and slice flesh.

7. Serve *Tilapia Ceviche* immediately with sliced avocado. Or refrigerate for 20 minutes and serve chilled.

Spicy Kale with Poached Eggs

Prep time: 10 minutes

Cook time: 12 minutes

INGREDIENTS

1 handful kale

2 cage-free eggs

1 small onion

1 clove garlic

1 tbsp extra virgin olive oil

¼ tsp ground black pepper

1 tsp low-sodium horseradish (optional)

INSTRUCTIONS

1. Chop the onion and mince the garlic. De-stem and wash the kale. Leaving a bit of water on the kale is ideal.

2. In a saucepan, add 1 tbsp extra virgin olive oil over medium heat. Add onion and cook until it begins to lose its opaqueness, about 5 minutes.

3. Add kale to saucepan and cover until kale is soft and green, about 5 minutes. Add garlic and stir, then cook another 2 minutes and remove from heat.

4. Fill a saucepan half full of water. Bring the water to a boil, then reduce heat below a boil and hold it there.

5. One by one, crack the eggs into a small cup or bowl and, with the lip of the cup or bowl close to the water's surface, dump the egg

into the water. If necessary, nudge the eggwhites closer to the yolks to keep them together.

6. Once all the eggs are in the water, remove the pan from heat and cover it. Let sit for 4 minutes until all eggs are cooked, then remove eggs from pan.

7. Place the greens on a plate and the two eggs on top of the greens. Top with horseradish if desired. Serve.

Smoked Salmon Bites

Prep Time: 10 minutes

Cook Time: N/A

Servings: 2

INGREDIENTS

1 large seedless cucumber

4 oz smoked salmon

1 avocado

½ red onion

1 Tablespoon lemon juice

1/2 teaspoon sea salt

Chives for garnish (optional)

INSTRUCTIONS

1. Slice the cucumber into ¾-inch thick slices.
2. Slice the smoked salmon into 1-inch by 1-inch pieces.
3. In a small bowl, mash the avocado with the salt, lemon juice, and onion.
4. Spread the avocado mash evenly across each of the cucumber slices.
5. Top each cucumber with a piece of the smoked salmon.
6. Garnish with a chive, if desired.

Basil Shrimp

Prep Time: 5 minutes

Cook Time: 20 minutes

Servings: 4

INGREDIENTS

1 pound shrimp, cleaned, tails on

1 Tablespoon coconut oil

1 bunch green onions, trimmed and chopped

1 cup fresh basil leaves

2 cloves garlic, sliced

2 Tablespoons lime juice

INSTRUCTIONS

1. In a large skillet, sauté the onions and garlic 2-3 minutes.
2. Add the shrimp and stir-fry for another 3-5 minutes, until cooked through.
3. Add the basil and lime juice and simmer another 2-3 minutes.

Turkey Apple Wraps

Prep Time: 5 minutes

Cook Time: N/A

Servings: 2

INGREDIENTS

8 ounces nitrite-free turkey lunch meat

1 apple, sliced into 8 spears

1 avocado, sliced into 8 pieces lengthwise

1 cup watercress

INSTRUCTIONS

1. Divide the turkey into fourths.
2. Lay one-fourth of the watercress, apple, and avocado lengthwise in the center of each piece of meat.
3. Roll up tightly and serve whole or slice each roll into bite-sized pieces.

Creamy Cauliflower Soup

Prep Time: 10 minutes

Cook Time: 20 minutes

Servings: 4

INGREDIENTS

1 large white onion, chopped

4 cloves garlic, minced

1 large head cauliflower, cored and chopped

4 cups chicken or vegetable stock

2 Tablespoons olive oil

4 strips bacon (optional)

1 teaspoon sea salt

INSTRUCTIONS

1. Sauté onion in olive oil in a large stockpot over medium-high heat until translucent (about 4 minutes).
2. Add the cauliflower, garlic, salt, and stock to the pot. Bring to a boil.
3. Reduce heat to low, cover, and simmer for 8-10 minutes.
4. While soup is simmering, pan fry the bacon strips (if using) until crispy.
5. Puree the soup with a hand blender, or blender.
6. Serve in bowls, crumbling the bacon on top.

Pineapple Jicama Salad

Prep Time: 5 minutes

Cook Time: N/A

Servings: 4

INGREDIENTS

1 small red onion, thinly sliced

2 cups jicama, peeled and diced

2 cups pineapple, peeled, cored, and chopped

4 cups red cabbage, shredded

2 Tablespoons lime juice

2 Tablespoons olive oil

½ cup fresh mint leaves

1 teaspoon sea salt

INSTRUCTIONS

1. In a bowl, combine the onion, jicama, pineapple, and mint.
2. In a separate bowl, whisk the olive oil, lime juice, and salt.
3. Serve the salad on a bed of red cabbage and drizzle the dressing over it before serving.

Sliced Veggie Spicy Chicken

Prep time: 4 minutes

Cook time: 8 minutes

Servings: 4

INGREDIENTS

4 pieces skinless grass-fed chicken thighs

1 onion

2 cloves garlic

3/4 cup sliced carrots

2 handfuls Kale greens

2 tbsp chinese five spice

2 tbsp smoked paprika

2 tbsp chipotle chili pepper powder

1 tbsp olive oil

2 tsp lemon juice

1 tbsp coconut oil

INSTRUCTIONS

1. Mince garlic and chop onion to desired size (medium strips work best). Chop carrots to 1/4" thickness. De-rib the kale and chop it coarsely, wash it and allow water to remain on the leaves. Bring 4 cups of water to a light boil.

2. Heat 1 tbsp olive oil over medium heat in a large pan. Add carrot and onion and cook for 8 minutes, stirring occasionally.

3. Meanwhile, heat 1 tbsp coconut oil over medium heat in a separate pan. Add chicken and cook for 4 minutes. Season chicken with chinese five spice, chipotle chili pepper powder and smoked paprika and turn, adding more of each spice to the other side of the chicken, cooking for another 4 minutes or until cooked through.

4. Add kale to boiling water and boil until bright green, about 5 minutes. Remove from water and let sit while the vegetables and chicken continue cooking.

5. Add everything into the pan with the vegetables and add 2 tsp lemon juice. Add minced garlic and stir for 1 minute.

6. Serve immediately.

No-Crust Pepper Quiche

Prep time: 5 minutes

Cook time: 3-6 minutes

INGREDIENTS

2 cage-free eggs

1 small onion

1 clove garlic

½ red bell pepper

1 tbsp extra virgin olive oil

¼ tsp smoked paprika

¼ tsp ground black pepper

INSTRUCTIONS

1. Finely chop onion, garlic and red bell pepper.
2. Pour extra virgin olive oil into a pan over medium heat.
3. Crack eggs and pour into a small bowl. Combine with onion, garlic and red bell pepper and whisk until mixed together.
4. Pour contents of bowl into pan and add smoked paprika and ground black pepper. Scramble until desired doneness.
5. Serve.

Uptown Clam Chowder

Prep Time: 10 minutes

Cook Time: 1 hour 15 minutes

Servings: 4

INGREDIENTS

24 - 36 medium live littleneck clams (or other clam varieties)

2 cans (11.5) organic tomato juice (or about 6 large tomatoes)

2 cans (14.5 oz) organic crushed tomatoes

2 medium carrots

2 medium celery stalks

2 medium parsnips

1 red bell pepper

1 tablespoon tamari (or coconut aminos or liquid aminos)

1 bay leaf

1/4 teaspoon cayenne pepper

1/2 teaspoon onion powder

1 tablespoon dried oregano

1 tablespoon dried basil

1 teaspoon dried thyme

1 teaspoon ground black pepper

Celtic sea salt, to taste

1 cup clam juice (or veggie or chicken stock, or water) (optional)

INSTRUCTIONS

1. Have fishmonger shuck clams. Or carefully shuck clams yourself. Reserve clam juice. Set aside in refrigerator.

2. Juice tomatoes, if using. Add tomato juice and crushed tomatoes to medium pot. Heat pot over high heat.

3. Remove seeds, stems and veins from bell pepper. Dice bell pepper, carrot, celery, and parsnips. Add to pot with spices and salt, to taste.

4. Bring pot to boil, then reduce heat to low. Place lid loosely over pot to prevent splatter. Simmer for 45 minutes. Stir occasionally.

5. Remove lid and stir. Add clam juice, stock or water to reach desired consistency (optional).

6. Remove clams from refrigerator and chop, if desired. Add clams and juice to pot. Stir to combine.

7. Replace lid and continue cooking about 20 - 30 minutes. Stir occasionally.

8. Transfer to serving dish and serve hot.

Chicken & Kale Soup

Prep Time: 10 minutes

Cook Time: 35 minutes

Servings: 4

INGREDIENTS

1 pound chicken breasts, cooked and shredded

6 cups chicken broth

1 large bunch kale, chopped

2 parsnips, peeled and diced

1 yellow onion, chopped

2 cloves garlic, sliced

2 Tablespoons olive oil

1 lemon, juiced

INSTRUCTIONS

1. Sauté onion in a large stockpot over medium-high heat in the olive oil until translucent, about 5 minutes.
2. Add the chicken, broth, kale, garlic, and parsnips. Bring to a boil. Lower heat, and simmer 20-30 minutes
3. Add the lemon juice just before serving

Sweet Guava Salad

Prep Time: 10 minutes*

Servings: 2

INGREDIENTS

2 ripe guavas

1 personal papaya (1 cup diced papaya flesh)

1 young coconut

1/2 teaspoon ground ginger (or 1/4 inch piece fresh ginger)

2 tablespoons fresh orange juice (about 1/2 orange)

INSTRUCTIONS

1. Dice guavas and add to medium mixing bowl. Peel papaya and cut in half, remove seeds and dice flesh. Remove coconut flesh from shell and dice. Add to bowl.
2. Juice orange into bowl and add ground ginger. Or peel fresh ginger and mince, then add to bowl. Toss to coat fruit evenly.
3. Transfer to serving dishes and serve immediately.
4. *Or refrigerate for 20 minutes and serve chilled.

Carrot Cranberry Crunch Salad

Prep Time: 5 minutes

Servings: 1

INSTRUCTIONS

2 large carrots

3 tablespoon dried cranberries

3 tablespoons raw almonds

1/2 small orange (or tangerine)

1/2 piece fresh ginger

1/2 teaspoon ground ginger

DIRECTIONS

1. Add carrots to food processor with shredding attachment and process, or grate with grater. Add to medium mixing bowl with cranberries and ground ginger.

2. Add almonds to food processor and pulse to coarsely chop. Or add to paper or plastic kitchen bag and pound with heavy rolling pin to crush. Peel ginger and dice or finely grate. Zest *then* juice orange. Add to carrot mixture and toss to combine.

3. Transfer to serving dish and serve immediately. Or refrigerate 20 minutes and serve chilled.

Made in the USA
Coppell, TX
06 March 2022

74562403R00031